Comfort

FOR THOSE WHO MOURN

CHUCK SMITH

CALVARY CHAPEL
PUBLISHING

P.O. Box 8000 • Costa Mesa, CA 92628 • (800) 272-WORD (9673) • www.twft.com

Comfort For Those Who Mourn
by Chuck Smith

© 1993, Calvary Chapel Publishing
P.O. Box 8000
Costa Mesa, CA 92628
(800) 272-WORD (9673)
Web Site: www.twft.com

Second printing 2001
Third printing 2009
Fourth printing 2010

ISBN: 978-0-936728-47-6

Unless otherwise indicated, all Scripture quotations are taken from the King James Version of the Bible. Translation emendations, amplifications, and paraphrases are by the author.

Printed in the United States of America.

"Blessed be the God and Father
of our Lord Jesus Christ,
which according to His abundant mercy
hath begotten us again
unto a lively hope by the resurrection
of Jesus Christ from the dead,
to an inheritance incorruptible,
and undefiled, and that fadeth not away,
reserved in heaven for you,
who are kept by the power of God
through faith."

1 Peter 1:3-5

FOR THOSE WHO MOURN

What is life? What is death? Is there life after death? These questions are buried deep in the mind of every man. We often push these questions into our subconscious, but they have a way of surfacing every now and then, and we usually mull them over for a while before we return them to the subconscious. Often these questions arise again at the death of a friend, a relative, or even a famous person. Severe mental or physical suffering can also arouse them. These questions have existed in the mind of man from the beginning. They are always there, begging for answers.

One of the oldest, if not the oldest, books in literary history is the book of Job. Here we find Job asking, "Where is man after he takes his last breath?" (Job 14:10) and, "If a man dies, does he go on living?" (Job 14:14). Job's questions arose from his grief over the death of his ten children in a tragic accident and out of his own intense suffering. But for Job, there were no answers.

Centuries later, "The Age of Philosophy" was born and men spent their entire lives seeking the answers to these questions. Still, by the end of that age, the philosophers had not come to any satisfactory answers.

Towards the end of the age of philosophy, Mary and Martha, two sisters who lived in the small village of Bethany, mourned the death of their brother. They had previously sent a message to Jesus asking Him to get there as quickly as possible, because the one He loved was deathly ill (John 11:1-3). Despite the urgency of this message, Jesus chose to relax at the Jordan River for a couple of days before beginning the two-day journey to Bethany, which lies on the Mount of Olives, on the wilderness side away from Jerusalem. By the time He approached the village with His disciples, His friend was dead. He had already been buried four days earlier.

When the sisters heard that Jesus was coming up the road from Jericho, Martha left the other mourners and ran to meet Him. As she came to Him, she exclaimed, "Jesus, if You had only been here earlier, my brother would not have died!" She was disappointed in Him. In a polite way she rebuked Him, saying, "What took You so long to get here? Lord, where were You when we needed You? Why didn't You respond to our prayers? You could have prevented death and averted our sorrow and grief. Why didn't You?" Isn't it interesting that we still ask Him the same questions today when a loved one dies?

Jesus answered Martha with comforting words: "Your brother will live again." Not fully understanding what He meant, Martha answered Him, "Yes, I know that, Lord, at the last day in the great resurrection." She must have been thinking of the prophecy in Daniel 12, where he speaks of the general resurrection of the dead; some would rise to everlasting life, others to everlasting contempt. But Jesus answered, "I am the resurrection, and the life: he that believes in Me, though he were dead, yet shall he live: and whosoever lives and believes in Me shall never die" (John 11:23-26).

Having made this radical statement, Jesus then asked Martha directly, "Do you believe this?" She answered, "Yes, Lord: I believe that You are the Christ, the Son of God." The statement Jesus made has to be one of the most radical any man in history has ever dared to make. If He were not the person who made the statement, it would immediately be cast off as

6

the vain babble of a fanatic. Imagine Napoleon telling his loyal troops before a battle, "If you believe in me, you will never die." Imagine if Hitler or even our own President had made that statement, you would immediately conclude that they were crazy and you probably wouldn't give it another thought. But because of who Jesus is, we cannot just pass over this radical remark. We must consider it seriously.

LIVING HOPE

When Jesus asked, "Do you believe this?" He immediately divided all mankind into two categories: those who believe and those who don't— those who have hope of life after death, and those who have no true hope for life after death. The apostle Peter said, "Blessed be the God and Father of our Lord Jesus Christ, which according to His abundant mercy has begotten us again unto a lively [living] hope by the resurrection of Jesus Christ from the dead, to an inheritance incorruptible, and undefiled, and that fades not away, reserved in heaven for you, who are kept by the power of God through faith" (1 Peter 1:3-5). Our hope of eternal life, according to Peter, is more than hope. It is a living hope verified by the resurrection of Jesus Christ.

At this point, you may logically argue, "If His words were true, why are there so many crosses on tombstones? What about all of the millions through the centuries who believed in Jesus and are now dead?" It is necessary to point out that the biblical definition of death is distinctly different from the dictionary definition. Medical science considers a man clinically dead when his brain ceases to function.

When a person lapses into a coma, life-support systems are hooked up, along with probes that allow doctors to observe brain wave activity. When the line on the monitor goes flat, that person is considered dead. Doctors often leave life-support systems on for another 24 hours. If the line remains flat, they remove the life-support and watch the monitor carefully for some flutter that would indicate the brain is calling for oxygen. If the line stays flat, they notify the family that their loved one is dead. The mind, or consciousness, has departed from the body, so the person is considered dead. Death by this definition is the separation of the consciousness from the body.

From a scriptural perspective, death is the separation of man's consciousness from God. If you are not conscious of God, the Bible declares that you are dead. Paul the apostle said that people living only for pleasure are dead while they are still alive (1 Timothy 5:6). God warned Adam in the garden that the day Adam ate the forbidden fruit he would surely die (Genesis 2:17). When Adam ate the fruit he died—spiritually.

Up to that time, God had fellowship with man in the garden. But after Adam ate the forbidden fruit, this fellowship with God was severed. Adam hid and God called to him, "Adam, where are you?" Adam, through sin, separated himself from God. His spiritual death would eventually lead to physical death. By believing in Jesus Christ we experience a spiritual birth. When Paul wrote to the believers in Ephesus, he said, "And you He quickened [made alive], who were dead in trespasses and sins" (Ephesians 2:1). Jesus said, "He that believes on the Son has everlasting life: and he that believes not the Son shall not see life; but the wrath of God abides on him" (John 3:36).

What Jesus was saying to Martha when He said, "If you live and believe in Me, you will never die," was that believers will never be consciously separated from God. I am so thankful that He did not mean that our conscious states would never leave our bodies. I cannot imagine a more horrible condition than remaining conscious long after my body could not adequately function. Wouldn't it be awful to be totally helpless; to be fed and bathed by someone you could not communicate with at all? To me that would be a fate worse than death.

BUILDING OF GOD

The Bible teaches that the "real me" is spirit. My body is a gift from God, a marvelous instrument through which I can express myself. Without our bodies, we could not relate to anything or anyone around us. What I am, what I think, what I feel; I relate to you through the medium of my body. You in turn, because of your body, can understand what I relate and in turn you relate to me. Because the body is the medium by which we relate, people will identify a person with their body. As we relate to one another, we familiarize ourselves and admire, appreciate, and love each other. We experience loving relationships, and that is exactly what God intended.

When our bodies, because of age, illness, accident or disease, can no longer relate what we are, what we feel or what we desire—when our bodies give us more pain than pleasure—they actually become prisons, incarcerating our spirits. Then it is time for God, in His love, to release our spirits from our bodies. The Scriptures say that those who believe in Jesus Christ do not experience death, they just go through a metamorphosis or change of body.

In 2 Corinthians 5:1 Paul describes that change this way: "We know that if our earthly house of this tabernacle were dissolved [our human bodies return to dust], we have a building of God, a house not made with hands, eternal in the heavens." To the believer then, death is nothing more than moving from a tent to a house! If you've ever been camping, you know what it's like to stay in a tent for any period of time. It is exciting and fun, but often inconvenient. But you can put up with the inconvenience because you know it is only temporary.

No one thinks of a tent as a permanent dwelling. Instead, they think of it as something transient. It is the same with our sojourns in these bodies. One day I will move out of my tent and into my mansion, my building of God, not made by hands, that Jesus has gone to prepare for me (John 14:1-2). You may read or hear someday that Chuck Smith died. Don't believe it. That will be poor reporting. It should be said that Chuck Smith moved from a worn-out tent into a beautiful mansion.

Paul went on to say that, as we live in these bodies, we often groan, earnestly desiring to be delivered or freed from our bodily restrictions. We do not desire to be spirits, but we want to move into our new heavenly bodies. He concludes, "We know that as long as we are living in our present bodies, we are absent from the Lord" (2 Corinthians 5:6). If we had our wish we would leave our earthly bodies so that we could be present with the Lord. Flesh and blood bodies cannot inherit the kingdom of heaven, so the move from tent to mansion is imperative. "This corruptible [my present body] must put on incorruption [my new body], and this mortal must put on immortality" (1 Corinthians 15:53).

This brings in a flood of new questions and speculations which Paul anticipates in 1 Corinthians 15. First of all, how are the dead raised and

9

what kind of bodies will they have when they come back with Christ? In 1 Thessalonians 4, Paul teaches that when the Lord comes to snatch His church away, He will bring with Him all of the saints that have already gone to be with Him. We will meet together in the air and be with Him forever.

For an answer to the question of how the dead are raised, Paul points to nature to illustrate the truth. Resurrection is not something unique or far-fetched; it is often demonstrated in nature. Every time a seed is planted, it dies before it comes forth in a new body and new life. This process is called germination. The very death of the seed is the process by which the new body comes forth. Paul is careful to point out, however, that the body that comes out of the ground is quite different than the body that was planted. We plant a bare grain, but God, through His miraculous recreative powers, gives it a new body that pleases Him. Paul tells us, "So also is the resurrection of the dead. It is sown in corruption, it is raised in incorruption: it is sown in dishonor, it is raised in glory: it is sown in weakness [our present feeble bodies], it is raised in power [our new glorified form]: it is sown a natural body [our present bodies, as a result of catabolic forces taking their toll], it is raised a spiritual body" (1 Corinthians 15:42-44).

But let's go a little further with Paul's illustration of the seed transformed into something new by death. If I held a scaly brown bulb before you and asked you what it was, you might carefully examine it and reply, "That's a gladiola, I think." Looking at that ugly thing, I might query, "A gladiola, are you sure?"

If I put the bulb in the soil and covered it with a little dirt, it would die and split. Out of that cleft a little white shoot would rise and turn green. As it continued to grow into a stalk, buds would emerge on the sides and open up into beautiful purple, or perhaps red variegated blossoms. Again I might ask you, "What is that gorgeous flower?"

Again you'd answer, "A gladiola."

I could object, saying, "A gladiola, you're putting me on! How can that beautiful flower be a gladiola when you just told me the brown scaly bulb was a gladiola?"

But it would be true. Though the bodies of the bulb and the flower are completely different, they are definitely related—the one sprang from the death of the other.

One day in heaven, you might see a handsome creature with an abundance of wavy brown hair. You might ask, "Who is that?" And when someone responds, "It's Chuck," you'll probably say, "Come on, you must be putting me on!" Not so. I simply will have blossomed into my new body, my building of God not made with hands.

In Paul's lesson on resurrection in 1 Corinthians 15, he asserts that even as we have borne the image of the earth and have been earthly, so shall we bear the image of the heavens. He is pointing out the fact that when God created these bodies to house our spirits, He made them out of the earth and He made them for the environmental conditions on Earth. It is true that the seventeen elements found in the soil are the same seventeen elements found in our bodies. God said to Adam, "Dust thou art, and unto dust shalt thou return" (Genesis 3:19).

Once, a little boy who was taught that same Scripture in Sunday school went home and looked under his bed and excitedly cried to his mother: "Come quick, there's someone under my bed and he's either coming or going!"

In the Psalms we are told that God knows our frame: that we are made out of dust (Psalm 103:14). My body was not just made out of earth, it was made for the Earth. My body was designed to extract oxygen from the atmosphere composed of 78.1% nitrogen, 20.9% oxygen and 1% aragon, carbon dioxide, and other trace gases. My body was designed to withstand fourteen pounds of pressure per square inch. My body was not made for any other place in our solar system, or as far as we know, any other place in our universe. If we want to take our bodies away from this planet, even a few thousand feet above it, we must take an artificial environment with us. Pilots that fly the SR71, a plane that can climb in excess of 80,000 feet above the earth, must wear pressurized suits with nitrogen and oxygen tanks. Without these suits, their body liquids would ooze out through their skin in less than a scant ten miles from the surface of the earth.

God has promised that, eternally, we will dwell with Him in His glorious kingdom. We don't know what the environmental conditions of heaven are, but there is no doubt that they are different from the conditions here; no doubt far superior. God could outfit us with space suits and let us clop clumsily around heaven, or He could give us totally new bodies designed to take us anywhere in the universe. God has wisely opted for the latter. He has prepared a mansion for me, a building of God not made with hands, eternal in the heavens. You may think that changing to a new body adapted to a totally different environment sounds far-fetched and incredible. Again we can turn to nature for illustrations that demonstrate the viability of this concept.

Look at the tadpole. By design it is limited to the water, yet when it goes through its metamorphosis and is transformed into a frog, it can now live on land also. Better yet, look at a fuzzy little caterpillar crawling across a field. I can imagine it trying to cross a highway in the summer with all its little feet on the hot black asphalt, thinking to itself, *How wonderful it would be if I could fly! I am so tired of hot dirty feet.* It might even attempt to fly by crawling up a tree, jumping off a limb and wiggling as fast as possible. But it's not aerodynamically designed for flight, so it will just fall to the ground.

One day, however, it may climb up the wall of your house, ooze a little natural glue to affix itself under your windowsill, spin a chrysalis and hang motionless for a while. If you were to squeeze that chrysalis, you would find an orange-yellow liquid inside. If you let it hang there though, and you watch it carefully, you will see it begin to twitch one day. It will jerk convulsively until beautiful orange-and black-wings unfurl and a new butterfly perches for a moment on its empty chrysalis. Then, without lessons or instructions, that Monarch butterfly will soon begin to fly around the yard, then over the fence and far away.

A metamorphosis from a body limited to crawling on the earth to one that can fly through the air is amazing. The new body allows the butterfly to exist in a whole new environment.

Sometimes as I look around at the chaos and sorrow on earth, I say, "Oh God, I am so tired of hot, dirty feet. I wish I could fly!" And one of these days, this corruption will put on incorruption, this mortal will put on immortality, and I will be changed in the twinkling of an eye (1 Corinthians 15:52-54). I will soar above the clouds to be with my God in the glories of His eternal kingdom, a world without end.

When I am gone, don't weep for me. I will be where my heart now longs to be, beholding the beauty of the face of the One I have never seen, yet I love. And though I don't see Him yet, I rejoice with unspeakable joy, full of glory (1 Peter 1:8). I discovered, through the death of my godly parents, that my great sorrow was not for them, but for myself, for my personal loss of the beautiful input they had in my life. My sorrow was selfish. I wasn't ready to let them go yet. I felt I still needed the security I always felt from their assurance and love. When I thought of them, there in His glorious presence, I rejoiced for them while I wept for myself.

Unless we are alive and remain until the coming of the Lord, we can be sure that one of these days, our spirits will leave our mortal bodies. Our friends might say we have died, but if we have lived and believed in Jesus, according to His promise we will have merely moved from our tents to our eternal homes where we will, as David, "dwell in the house of the Lord forever" (Psalm 23:6).

We will have blossomed like the gladiola, and we will soar in our new environment like the butterfly. Thank God this is our living hope, guaranteed by the resurrection of Jesus Christ from the dead!

LESSONS FROM DAVID
In 2 Samuel 1 we find David receiving word of the death of his dear friend, Jonathan, and of King Saul, whom he admired so greatly. In observing how David deals with his grief, there are some important lessons we can learn. Sooner or later every one of us will experience the grief and sorrow of having lost someone whom we loved very dearly. It could be that we lose them in death. It could be that we just lose them as a close relationship drifts apart. But the loss of someone that we love can be an extremely devastating experience. Many people have been totally destroyed because of their inability to deal with grief.

Upon hearing the news, we read that David first responded emotionally, demonstrating his grief by tearing his clothes. Although that might seem strange to us, during the time of David it was common to rend a garment as an expression of extreme sorrow. David then fasted, wept and mourned until evening. It is important to understand that releasing our sorrows is a very beneficial thing to do. Often we feel that we must put on a brave face and repress any public expression of grief. Some even feel that they are being spiritual by doing so. But to release our emotions and shed some tears is not at all bad. In fact, it is quite therapeutic.

David's expression of grief was not limited to tears. He then spent some time reflecting on the lives of Jonathan and Saul and wrote a type of elegy called a lamentation for them. It begins as David declares,

> The beauty of Israel is slain upon thy high places: how are the mighty fallen! Tell it not in Gath, publish it not in the streets of Askelon; lest the daughters of the Philistines rejoice, lest the daughters of the uncircumcised triumph. Ye mountains of Gilboa, let there be no dew, neither let there be rain, upon you, nor fields of offerings: for there the shield of the mighty is vilely cast away, the shield of Saul, as though he had not been anointed with oil. From the blood of the slain, from the fat of the mighty, the bow of Jonathan turned not back, and the sword of Saul returned not empty. Saul and Jonathan were lovely and pleasant in their lives, and in their death they were not divided: they were swifter than eagles, they were stronger than lions. Ye daughters of Israel, weep over Saul, who clothed you in scarlet, with other delights; who put on ornaments of gold upon your apparel. How are the mighty fallen in the midst of the battle! O Jonathan, thou was slain in thine high places. I am distressed for thee, my brother Jonathan: very pleasant hast thou been unto me: thy love to me was wonderful, passing the love of women. How are the mighty fallen, and the weapons of war perished! (2 Samuel 1:19-27).

In these beautiful and poetic words, David gave expression to the deep grief he was feeling. The people of Israel were able to sing these words in tribute to their fallen king and his son.

The third way that David dealt with his grief was quite interesting, and on the surface perhaps a little difficult to understand. Verse 18 says that David gave orders that each father in Judaea was to teach his children how to use a bow. It is significant to note that in a time of emotional distress, David instructed the people to get involved in a constructive activity. In a time of grief and sorrow, people often make the mistake of becoming almost paralyzed by a morbid kind of introspection and emotional indulgence. This approach is not only unhealthy, but actually intensifies and prolongs the grief. An important part of overcoming sorrow is to become active, to learn a new skill, to develop a new hobby, or to get out and travel.

David instructed his people to teach their children how to use a bow. Now, they didn't have sporting goods stores in those days. They couldn't just go downtown and buy an archery set. First they had to find a tree that had a good sturdy branch, cut it down and carve the branch out into the bow. They also had to look for branches that were straight that they could fashion into arrows. Then they had to find the feathers and tie them on to each arrow. It was a real process in just making an archery set for the children.

There was a very important benefit that was derived from David's order. Think of the closeness that was developed between the fathers and their children as they worked together on this project. I remember years ago when I taught my sons how to use a bow. Of course, we went to a sporting goods store and bought a couple of archery sets for them, including the targets and the bale of hay. First I taught my sons how to string the bow properly. Then I taught them how to notch the arrow in the string the proper way, how to accurately sight the target, and how to release the arrow at the proper time. I had purchased bows that were a little stronger than what they could immediately pull, so in the beginning of their lessons I had to reach around behind them and help them as they drew back on the bow. As we worked on this activity together we found it to strengthen our love for one another.

So we can see that David's real purpose was to strengthen the family bonds within Israel. Not only would archery take the people's minds off the loss of their leaders, it would also serve to bring parents and children closer to one another. Clearly, in a time of loss, we also should seek to strengthen the bonds within our families. We should make an effort to pursue activities that can draw the family together.

We also see tremendous foresight on the part of David. He was taking lessons from the past and making them a valuable asset for the future. In battle, the Philistines introduced a new form of warfare. The bow and the arrow were used in a tightly organized, concerted effort. Bows and arrows had often been used in battle, but for the first time all the archers were concentrating on a single target. If a hundred arrows are being shot at the same target, some of them are going to get through. You can't dodge them all, nor can you use the shield to deflect them all. It was this new concentrated approach that resulted in the mortal wounding of Saul. David immediately saw the advantages of this long-distance form of warfare.

King Saul was a powerful warrior. In David's lament he noted that the sword of Saul did not return empty. In one-on-one, hand-to-hand combat, the Philistines didn't stand a chance against Saul. So they cleverly adjusted their strategy. The archers brought Saul down from a safe distance, a lesson in tactics that wasn't lost on David. This would not be the last battle Israel would face. In fact, at that time in history, warfare with various roving tribes was a fact of life. Many times the people would have to arise to defend village and family against attackers. David could see that it would be an advantage if they could develop archery skills for the future. Learning from the lessons of the past he now makes a practical application for the future. He ordered that fathers teach their children the use of the bow.

Beyond it being a more efficient form of civil defense, this practice also served as a very fitting memorial for Jonathan. Now, I have never really been impressed by memorials that are made in stone. We have all seen plaques or marble monuments that declare all the wonderful things a deceased person had done. While I am sure these have meaning for friends and relatives, I believe there is a better way to honor the memory of those who have passed on. How much more significant it would be to look at the life of a person and attempt to emulate the strengths and skills that made them special.

You see, Jonathan was a noted archer. In his lament, David speaks of the bow of Jonathan. Every time the fathers were out with their children teaching them how to use a bow they would remember Jonathan as a mighty man and an outstanding warrior. It was an extremely fitting tribute to

Jonathan to teach the children the use of the bow. And how beautiful it is to honor those loved ones who have passed on by remembering and emulating their strengths.

WITNESSES

My dad was an outstanding witness for Jesus Christ. As far as personal witnessing, he was one of the best. He was constantly sharing with people. I can't remember him ever meeting a person without turning the encounter into an opportunity to share the love of Jesus. He was tremendously gifted with the knack, the capacity, and the zeal to witness in almost any situation. I can remember many years ago our family had a little trailer that we pulled behind a Model-A Ford, and every summer we would go on a camping trip to Yosemite National Park. It was great; we really enjoyed it. But then in 1934, Airstream came out with a very nice, light travel trailer. Dad went down and bought one, and boy, we stepped up in the world! Now we had a better trailer, and our camping trips became very expansive. We went all over the western part of the United States.

On one trip we visited the Redwoods in Northern California. We had eaten dinner and were settled down for the night. We had just turned off the Coleman lantern, and the light was gradually going out. We had all bedded down and were quite cozy when there was a knock on the door of the trailer. Dad opened the door and there was a state trooper standing there. He said, "You know, you can't park here. It's against the law. You'll have to get off the road someplace. If you go up the road about two miles, and go back in about ten miles, there is a beautiful place to camp. Hardly anyone knows about it, it's so far off the road, but for a dollar you can connect up to the electricity. There's a nice stream, and in the morning you can go swimming."

So we drove up the road and pulled off and went way back into the woods. Dad went in to make arrangements to get a spot to park the trailer and it seemed that he was gone a long time. Mom finally decided to see what had happened and there was dad sharing Jesus with a man he met at the campsite. Soon the man got down on his knees and accepted the Lord. Afterwards the man told us, "I can't believe this! My parents were always witnessing to me. I got so sick of them telling me that I needed the Lord and that I needed Jesus Christ. I decided to get as far away from people as possible so that no one would ever witness to me again. That is why I bought this place way back here in the sticks. Now here you are!" And my dad said, "Well, just shows you, you'll never escape the Lord. You can run as far as you want, but you might as well give your heart to Him, because you are never going to escape Him." And Dad led him to the Lord. But that's just the way my dad was.

So when the Lord saw fit to take Dad home, I determined that I would learn the skills of witnessing. He was skillful. His bow was witnessing. And so I determined that I was going to learn the use of the bow—witnessing for the Lord—and that I might become a more effective witness for the Lord. Rather than just sitting back and weeping, and saying, "Oh, my dad. I miss my dad," and plunging into self-pity because I lost my dad and brother, I decided to take something that they were able to do well, something in which they set a good example, and develop that skill.

My mother was a woman of prayer. I cannot remember waking up a single morning, but the first thing I heard was my mother out in the other room praying. She would get up an hour or so before the rest of the family and spend the first couple of hours in prayer. I can't remember going to sleep at night, but the last thing I'd heard as I would drift off to sleep was my mother in the other room praying. What a blessing it was to grow up in a home surrounded by prayer. My mother was one of the most godly, praying women I've ever met. When the Lord saw fit to take her home, I thought, *I'm going to develop my skills in praying. I'm going to give myself more to prayer. I'm going to learn to pray as she prayed. I'm going to learn the use of that "bow."*

This was David's intent as he desired to honor Jonathan's life. He ordered everyone to teach their children how to use the bow. It was as if he was saying to Israel, "This man has set a classic example; let's follow it." And it became a living memorial to him. When the time comes and we lose those who have been so influential, those who have touched our lives, it's good to get active. It is good to take something that they have been skillful or adept in, and determine that we are going to develop that ourselves, following the good example that they have left.

Clearly in David's time a bow was a weapon of warfare. And in a sense we can see this passage as instructive for the spiritual battles we fight, especially those that involve the use of the spiritual weapon of prayer. The Bible says that the weapons of our warfare are not carnal, but they are mighty through God for the pulling down of the strongholds of the enemy (2 Corinthians 10:4). And whereas the bow was able to lob the arrows and strike the enemy from a distance, without this close hand-to-hand combat, so prayer can work the same way.

I like to think of our prayers as an excellent weapon by which we can bring a spiritual influence upon people from a distance. Many of us know what hand-to-hand spiritual warfare is like. We've witnessed so much to those we love because we are so desirous that they know Jesus, the joy of following Him, and the assurance of eternal life. We so desperately want them to know the glorious love of God and the power of Jesus Christ in their lives, that sometimes we can get a little pushy. And sometimes people begin to resent our witnessing to them. They say, "Give me a break! Stay off my case! Don't talk to me about this anymore! We can't talk about religion without arguing, so please don't talk to me!" And it seems that all our best efforts have done is to slam the door of witness shut! At times like that it is great to know that God has equipped us with the long-distance weapon of prayer.

Rather than forcing a confrontation, we can just start shooting the arrows from a distance. They start getting hit and they don't even know where it came from. They start feeling conviction for their sin. They start feeling miserable. "Why do I feel bad about that? I do it all the time. I know it's not right, but why do I feel so horrible?" The Spirit begins to work in their hearts as we through prayer can bind the work of the enemy. We through prayer can open their hearts to the things of the Spirit of God. And prayer becomes a tremendous instrument in spiritual warfare in bringing others into the light and into the knowledge and understanding of our Lord.

There was a lady who lived in St. Louis, Missouri who was a beautiful Christian. Her husband was a lawyer, a man of keen intellect. He had been elected to Congress and sat in the House of Representatives. As was her habit, she met with a group of ladies for prayer. And on one particular Tuesday morning in March, she and her friends decided that they were going to pray for her husband's salvation every morning at ten o'clock. Though he was a wonderfully intelligent man, he was an agnostic and was very resistant to all her attempts at witnessing to him.

So every morning she and the ladies would meet and at ten o'clock, shoot their arrows towards Washington D.C. They would pray that somehow God would speak to his heart, and that He would bring to his heart a realization of his need for God. It was a very busy session of Congress, but when it finally recessed, he returned home to Missouri. On Saturday morning he asked her, "Are you going to go to church tomorrow?" She said, "Well, if it's alright with you, I would like to go to church." He said to her, "Do you mind if I go with you?" She was absolutely shocked! "I'd love to have you go with me."

So the next morning he went to church with her, and when the invitation was given, he went forward. That day at lunch they were sharing together how glorious it was that God had now united them completely. Even though they had had a good marriage from an emotional and physical standpoint, there was a missing spiritual ingredient that had now been made complete. They could hardly believe the joy and blessing they now shared, and the congressman was thrilled by the joy and peace he was experiencing.

As they were sharing she said, "Well, Honey, last March I asked the ladies in my prayer group to join with me in prayer for you, that God would bring you to receive Christ." He asked, "When did you start?" She said, "Well, it was the second Tuesday morning in March. Let's get the calendar out." They got the calendar out, and found the exact date and time that they had started. He pulled out the daily journal that he kept and said, "I want you to see what I wrote on March 12th at noon."

And there in his ledger, written in the midst of a busy, heated session of Congress were the words, "Suddenly, I have come to an amazing awareness that I need God in my life." Those arrows of prayer were hitting home. Just as David decided to make the use of the bow and arrow a priority for the people of Israel, we need to make the use of the bow of prayer a priority in our own lives, that we might be effective for God in the spiritual battle in which we are all engaged.

We all know the pain of losing someone we love, but rather than allowing sorrow and grief to rule our lives, we can turn even a time of tragedy into a growing experience when we give it to God. The name Alexander Cruden probably doesn't mean anything to you. However, if I would say, "*Cruden's Concordance*," then a lot of you would nod and say, "Oh yes, of course. I use *Cruden's Concordance*. I find it a tremendous advantage and help in finding Scriptures." What many people don't know is that *Cruden's Concordance* was more or less born out of a very sad experience in the life of this man. He was deeply in love with a young girl who jilted him, but rather than just closing in around himself, and moaning and groaning, he decided that he would devote his life to setting up this concordance so that people could find Scriptures more easily. And *Cruden's Concordance* was actually born out of that tragedy.

The story is told of a wealthy man in Venice, who sat in his room day by day mourning over life. He was convinced that life had no meaning or purpose. Finally he had sunk so low in despair that he decided to drown himself in the Venice Canal. As he was on his way to end it all, a little boy came up and tugged on his pants leg and asked him for some money. He said, "My family hasn't eaten for three days! We're hungry! Can you give me a little money?" The man was skeptical and didn't believe the story of the little boy. But he said, "Take me to your house." So the little boy took him to meet his family. He saw that it had in fact been days since they had eaten. So he emptied out all of the money that he had in his pockets. And when he saw the joy that came upon these people who now had money to eat, he thought, *Now that's worth living for!* And he spent the rest of his life helping the poor in Venice.

It is very easy to close ourselves off and say, "Oh, life isn't worth living." Grief or loss can cause us to isolate ourselves in a prison of sadness. Powerful emotions like grief can destroy our lives—or be used by God as stepping stones to reach out in a new dimension, a new life, a new talent, or a new capacity. We can discover that God has a lot in store for us. The death of a loved one is not the end—it's just a turn in the road to a whole new path that God might have for us. When we take a time of tragedy and use it as an opportunity to learn to use a "bow," there is no telling what wonderful things God will do!

As those whom we love—those who have meant so much—are suddenly taken from us, the sorrow can either bring an end to life or be a stepping stone into greater horizons. It all depends on how we respond. David showed us the proper response. God help us to do the same. Maybe some of you are in a hole today. Maybe some of you have been grieving for a long time. Hey, it's time to quit sitting still. Let's learn to use a "bow."

Thank You, Lord, for the living hope that we have through the resurrection of Jesus from the dead and for an inheritance that is incorruptible and undefiled and fades not away, that is reserved in heaven for us, that is kept in Your power. Minister today, Lord, unto each of our hearts concerning life—our life in Christ.

As Paul the apostle declared, "For me to live is Christ, and to die is gain" (Philippians 1:21). Lord, we look for that day when we too shall gain the glory of Your presence. Keep us, Lord, through the power of Your Spirit. Let us continue to walk in fellowship with You until that day when You call for us. In Jesus' name, we pray. Amen.

Therefore my heart shall rest in hope, for You have shown to me the path of life. In Your presence is fullness of joy and at Your right hand there are pleasures forever more (Psalm 16:11).

SINNER'S PRAYER

If you want a personal relationship with God and the assurance that your sins have been forgiven, here is a suggested prayer:

> Father, I come to You, confessing my sin and asking for Your forgiveness. I thank You, Lord, for You have promised that if I will confess my sins, You will be faithful to forgive me and cleanse me from all unrighteousness. I want to turn from my sins and live in a way that will please You. And so I ask for Your help, Lord. I ask that You give me the power through Your Holy Spirit to live the right way.
>
> I thank You that Jesus Christ died on the cross, paying the price for my sins, and then rose from the dead. I accept Him now as my Savior, my Lord, and my friend.
>
> I also thank You, because You've said that whoever comes to You, You will in no way cast out. Thank You for giving me a new life in Christ. I surrender myself to You. Make me what You want me to be, in Jesus' name. Amen.

WHAT NEXT?

If you have decided to accept Jesus Christ as your Savior, you are now born again. Here are a few things that will help you to grow as a Christian:

1. PRAY—Prayer is like a telephone line that goes directly to God. It's important to spend time talking to Him every day, the more the better (Philippians 4:6).

2. READ THE BIBLE—The Bible is like a love letter from God. The more you read it, the more you'll fall in love with Him (1 Peter 2:2).

3. FELLOWSHIP—You need to have friends who share your beliefs and who can encourage you. This is why it's so important to find a good, Bible-believing church where you can meet other Christians (Hebrews 10:24-25).

4. WITNESS TO OTHERS—Share your faith in Jesus Christ with others. Pray that the Lord will reveal how and when you should witness (Mark 16:15).

If you need help finding a church in your area, feel free to call us at Calvary Chapel Costa Mesa, California. Our staff can help you locate a good place to fellowship. Our phone number is (714) 979-4422 and we are available between the hours of 8:00 a.m. and 5:00 p.m., Pacific Standard Time.

Also, here are some websites that can help you:

www.calvarychapel.com/gospel

www.calvarychapel.com/costamesa/
newbelievers/study/index.htm

www.twft.com

www.calvarychapel.com

God bless you and we pray that you continue
to grow closer to the Lord every day!

ABOUT THE AUTHOR:

Chuck Smith, senior pastor at Calvary Chapel Costa Mesa, California, has been a Bible teacher for more than sixty years.

His Bible studies can be heard weekdays on the international radio program, *The Word For Today*. His books include *Living Water, Why Grace Changes Everything, Final Act, Love The More Excellent Way, Wisdom For Today, and Prayer Our Glorious Privilege*.

CALVARY CHAPEL
PUBLISHING

P.O. Box 8000 • Costa Mesa, CA 92628 • (800) 272-WORD (9673) • www.twft.com